Grandpa's 51 RULES OF THE ROAD
FOR BEGINNER DRIVERS

By Leonard P. Zimmerman Sr.

Edited by Charmain Zimmerman Brackett

Illustrations and design by
Leonard "Porkchop" Zimmerman

INTRODUCTION

It would be a lot simpler if there were no other cars and trucks on the road while learning to drive; however, we know that's not the case. Be that as it may, these rules should give some insight as to what you need to look out for while driving.

LOOK OUT... these are key words, not only when learning how to drive, but when driving as a seasoned veteran. You can never assume that the other driver is going to always abide by the law 100 percent of the time. It just doesn't work that way, and you need to learn that one up front.

I always believed that doing what I learned to be correct and looking out for the other guy would keep me safe. Needless to say after more than 55 years of driving this has proven to be effective for me. You can be a GOOD DRIVER, but you have to have that edge. Being observant to the condition of the road and looking out for other drivers will keep your insurance rates down as well as avoiding accidents.

The 51 rules are a compilation of years of close calls. I don't pretend to have all the answers. There are plenty of Grandpas and Grandmas out there who can add to this list. In fact, if there is a sequel to this RULE BOOK, I'll need support from you readers. Send me your rule, and if it is accepted, your name and state will be placed at the bottom of the page. Write to: Grandpa's Rules, P.O. Box 1434, Augusta, Georgia 30903.

Some of my students are out on the road, and they are doing well. *They should;* **Grandpa taught them.**

(Let's go!)

RULE 1

The driver is like the Captain of a ship; passengers must obey or exit the vehicle.

RULE 2

The first thing you need to do is buckle your seat belt and see that everyone else
is secured.

RULE 3

Check mirrors for proper vision and make certain all doors are closed. Turning a corner and having a door open isn't copacetic.

RULE

4

LOOK, LOOK, and *LOOK* Some More.

Look
before you put your car
into gear and start driving.

Look
before you change lanes.

Look
before you go on a green light.

Look
before you pass a school bus.

Look
before you go over a
railroad crossing.

RULE
5

Find the speed limit for the zone you're driving in. You can always go slower!

RULE
6

Observe the vehicles around you at all times. If a car behind you suddenly disappears, it either turned off the road or is passing you. *Keep alert.*

RULE 7

Just because a car has a directional signal on, doesn't mean the driver is going to turn. Sometimes, they even turn the opposite direction of the signal.

RULE 8

Don't talk on your cell phone or text while driving. Use it for emergencies, but only if you are pulled off the road and into a safe place.

RULE 9

Do not tailgate the vehicle in front of you. You're liable to have their bumper mounted on your grill.

RULE
10

If someone is tailgating you, pull into a safe area and let them pass. Better to be safe than rear-ended.

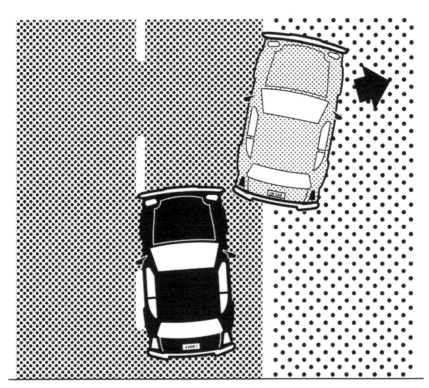

RULE
11

When confronted with elderly drivers, give them the right-of-way. *Chances are they are going to take it anyway.*

RULE 12

Size does matter.
If a vehicle is larger than the one you're driving, getting in its way can only make you dead right.

RULE
13

If you are sitting at a light and the vehicle to either side is blocking your vision, allow those vehicles to move first when the light turns green.

RULE 14

Traffic lights should be obeyed by everyone, but that doesn't mean they always are. Before moving into an intersection, make sure it's safe.

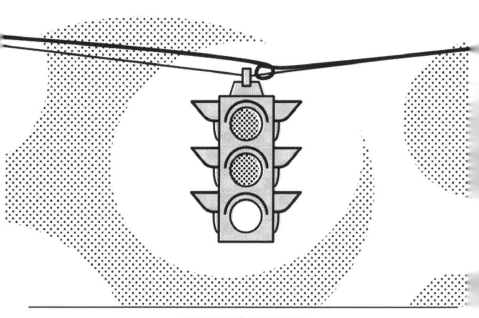

RULE
15

Watch the vehicle in front of you. If it swerves suddenly or taillights come on, slow down and be careful. Evaluate the situation, and take defensive action if necessary.

RULE
16

When you are observing traffic farther down the road, don't get such a fixation that you lose track of what is taking place in front of you.

RULE
17

Stay in the center of your lane while driving. Getting too close to the right or left might open a chance for an unexpected surprise. Cars might attempt to pass you.

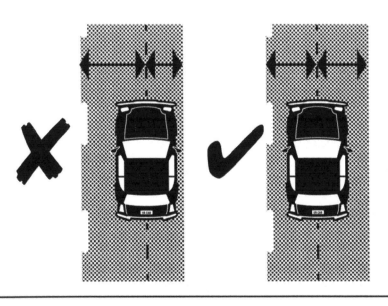

RULE 18

You should always carry a set of jumper cables with you and learn how to use them. Plus, make sure the spare tire is inflated, and carry a jug of water just in case.

RULE
19

KNOW your vehicle.

Know
how to put gas in the tank.

Know
how to check fluid levels such as oil, transmission, and brake fluids.

Know
how to check tire pressure and how to fill your tires.

Know
how to change a tire.

RULE 20

Road signs are for your benefit. Construction zone fines double in some states. Obeying the rate of speed for exiting a freeway will keep you on the road. Hazardous conditions exist when you choose to disobey posted road signs.

RULE 21

If you have a mechanical problem or run out of gas, pull onto the shoulder of the road. Don't stop in the middle of the road, you are asking for trouble.

RULE 22

When you stop at a street corner, do so behind the white line. This will keep the nose of the car out of the intersection. Being nosy can be costly.

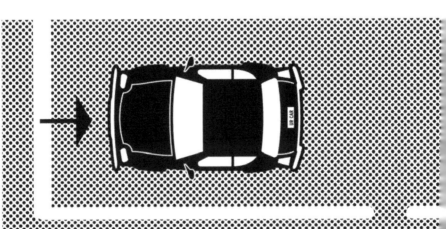

RULE
23

Come to a complete stop when approaching a red light or stop sign. Don't roll through it; there could be another car coming.

RULE 24

Smokers should never throw a lighted cigarette out the window. It could cause a roadside fire or blow back into the vehicle.

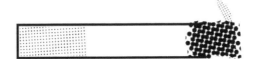

RULE
26

If you get sleepy behind the steering wheel, the best thing to do is to pull into a safe place and take a break.
A quick fix of coffee or opening the window for fresh air are only temporary measures.

RULE
27

Your right foot is used for the accelerator. Your right foot is also used for the brake. The left foot is for keeping the beat with the music.

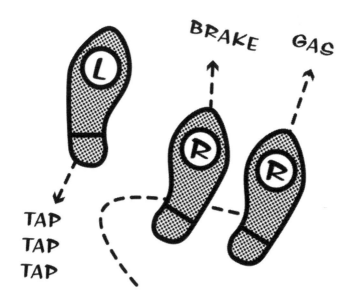

FOR BEGINNER DRIVERS

RULE 28

Keep the sun visor in the up position unless you're trying to block the sun. A down sun visor could restrict your vision at the wrong time.

RULE
29

Always make sure you have your driver's license, car registration, and car insurance information with you.

FOR BEGINNER DRIVERS

RULE
30

Never, Never, Never, Never leave the scene of an accident. Doing so will only make matters worse.

RULE 31

If you are involved in an accident, don't fall for the story, *"Let's settle this ourselves and keep the insurance companies from raising our premiums."*

The individual may not have insurance.

You need a police report for your claim.

The person may be trying to con you for other reasons.

FOR BEGINNER DRIVERS

RULE 32

Keep an extra set of car keys with you.

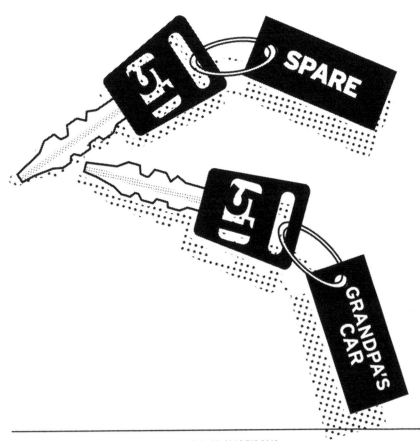

RULE
33

If you run out of gas, whose fault is it? Check your gauges before starting off.

RULE 34

Your car is not a beauty salon. Don't put on your makeup while driving.

RULE 35

If you are trying to be cool behind the wheel, turn on the air conditioner. The vehicle is not a toy. Sit up straight, put both hands on the wheel, and watch the road. The right people will see you.

THIS IS NOT A TOY.

FOR BEGINNER DRIVERS

RULE
36

When driving in a parking lot at the mall or a shopping center, drive slowly and keep your eyes on the road. Watch for pedestrians and other cars. Sometimes, they are paying more attention to their packages than the other cars.

RULE
37

Pedestrians don't always pay attention when crossing at a light. Don't assume people will stop on red and walk on green. A "do not walk" sign doesn't always register with pedestrians. Proceed with caution through a cross walk.

RULE 38

Watch out for bicyclists and motorcycles. Remember the vehicle you are driving can be a lethal weapon.

RULE
39

When you are learning to drive, keep your window open on the driver's side. Get accustomed to the sounds of the other vehicles around you. Sometimes you can't see a vehicle, but you can hear it.

RULE
40

Always keep your eyes on the road. Eye to eye contact with an individual is important in business. It always applies to driving. Keep your hands on the wheel, and your eyes on the road.

RULE
41

It's good to have a towing service on your insurance policy or a towing service plan from some other agency.

RULE 42

If you get stopped by the police, don't be a smart aleck. Show respect, and you'll get respect. If you show respect and don't get it, remember the rule. Don't get smart.

RULE
43

If you get
a speeding
ticket, whose
fault is it?

RULE
44

Trying to beat a red light is like playing Russian roulette. You'll win sometimes, but when you lose, how costly will it be?

RULE
45

Observe off-ramp speed signs. They are there for a reason. If you exceed the speed posted, you may lose control of your car or worse.

RULE
46

The "no passing" line painted on the road means just that. You can't see over a hill or around a curve. Passing when you are not supposed to may end your driving career and your life.

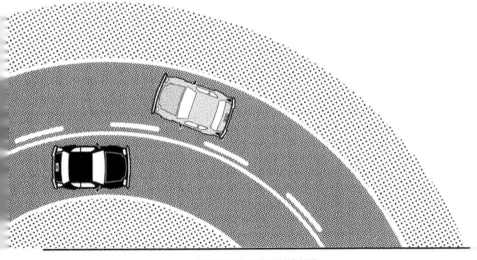

RULE 47

Parking lights are for parking not for driving around in the middle of the night.

RULE
48

Both hands go on the wheel. Running over a pothole in the street, having a blow-out in your tire, hydroplaning on water, or driving on ice can't be handled with just one finger if you lose control. Be safe. Use both hands at all times.

RULE
49

Watch out for tractor trailers and other vehicles that carry things, such as

- Gravel trucks • Log trucks
- Wreckers and tow trucks
- Garbage trucks

These are a few. Items can fly out of some of these vehicles and hit your car.

RULE
50

When parking on a hill or grade, use the emergency brake, and take the key of the car with you. You should never leave the keys in the car at any time.

RULE 51

If your Grandpa is teaching you how to drive, don't argue with him. He is apparently the one who loves you enough to sit in the front seat of the car while you're learning to drive.

Dedication

Putting *Grandpa's 51 Rules* together was a family effort. I'd like to thank my children for their help. My son, Leonard "Porkchop" Zimmerman, used his talent and sense of humor to create the illustrations, and my daughter, Charmain Zimmerman Brackett, made sure the words flowed together and the commas were in all the right places.

I especially want to thank my wife, Nona, for her support all these years.

And I want to give Ashlee Henry a shout-out for her help in the technical aspects of getting this together.

NOTES

Notes

Notes

Made in the USA
Columbia, SC
15 December 2020